Transforming Matter

Also by Donna Hilbert

Poetry:

Deep Red

Mansions

Triple Exposure

Fiction:

Waiting for My Baby

*Women Who Make Money
and the Men Who Love Them*

DONNA HILBERT

Transforming Matter

Pearl
Editions

LONG BEACH, CALIFORNIA

The author would like to thank the editors of the following publications, in which some of these poems have appeared, often in different form or under another title: *Black Buzzard Review, Chiron Review, Pearl, Rosebud, Sycamore Roots*. In England, *Blade, Fire, Staple, Tears in the Fence, The North*. A number of poems are among those collected under the title *Code Green* and appearing as a special section of *Pearl*, or in the chapbook *Feathers and Dust*, published by Event Horizon Press.

The inscription quoted in the poem "In Quintana Roo" is from a painting by Malena Alvarez.

Thanks to Linda Ewing and Jill Young who read everything early and often and whose advice and support is priceless.

Thanks also to Tere Sievers, Joan Merrill, Patti Harvey, Moe and Debbie Shahbani who have graciously carried me on their shoulders.

Library of Congress Catalog Number: 99-64733

ISBN 1-888219-14-9

Cover illustration by Jennifer Kaufman

Book design by Marilyn Johnson

PEARL EDITIONS
3030 E. Second Street
Long Beach, California 90803
U.S.A.

This book is for my husband, Larry Hilbert,
who was killed in the midst of joy
on August 25, 1998.

Contents

IV. ANIMAL, VEGETABLE, MINERAL

V. GRIEF BECOMES ME

VI. TIME, SPACE

I. Six Genre ∽

Novel

Anna under the train,
Emma's apothecary poison,
while my late-twentieth century
life meanders, lacks plot.
Character and conflict
appear in abundance and on cue,
but I shrink from the climax,
not wanting the denouement
to occur without me.

Short Story

It's true. The end
and beginning are hard,
but in between is bliss—
the gold coin of revelation—
with no further chapter
in which the piper appears
demanding to be paid,
for the unconsidered slap,
the awful kiss.

Poem

I throw my shoulder
out of socket hurtling
lightning from the dark
portentous clouds.
It's not enough
to touch the gods,
I want to be one.
I think I am, in fact,
levitating here with you
while below us children cry
and want their supper.

Movie

In this re-make
the plot is hackneyed
but well-wrought
and the star turns reverse for twist:
she refuses to leave her husband
while he fears he's just an object used
for sex.
Distraught, she tumbles
from plot point to plot point
praying *deus ex machina*
save me. Save me.

Play

Better to rise and fall
in one act.

Problems with the second
are classic:
Everyone on stage to explain—
no ecstasy, all exposition.

What is sadder than the curtain
on act three?
Extra time, to be sure,
but we fall on the sword
just the same.

Opera

Every night while I cook dinner
Mimi dies
in grand voice, consumptive
under a blood-spumed Paris moon.

How can there be more suffering than this?

Every night to die for passion,
yet be forced alive
assigned the living task of chopping onion,
smashing buds of garlic with a spoon.

II. Person, Place, Thing

Queens

I loved the flat sassy
bodies of my paper dolls:
movie queens,
hands on hips,
lips in a frozen pout,
glamour pusses
in tab-on fur capes.
More, I loved cardboard
Dale Evans,
Queen of the Cowgirls,
in her fringed suede jacket
and high-strutting boots.
Days, she rode Buttermilk
roping outlaws with Roy.
At sundown,
when she clicked her spurs,
buttermilk biscuits popped
from her oven. She sopped
them in syrup,
fed them to Roy.
Dale never got sticky,
never dropped a crumb,
never wore an apron,
was never jealous of Trigger
who shared their bed
whinnying and snorting
till sun up.

The Swimmer

Brown hair stuffed in a cap
strapped under my chin, I swam
through junior high summers
at the Reseda Park pool,
in water heavy with chlorine.
All summer I smelled
like the sink
Mother sprinkled with Comet
before leaving for work.

Maxine's mom was a dry cleaner.
Days off, she cadged
invitations to swim
in backyard pools of the rich
whose clothes she pressed,
steamed in her shop.
Mother said she was nervy
just like Maxine. Like Maxine,
her hair was curly, dark.

Days after swimming,
we dipped crackers
in mustard, Worcestershire,
any liquid found in their kitchen
went into our sauce,
an extra-strength potion.
We dipped, ate, were transformed
into amazing girls:
scientists, swimmers.

At school in September:
Whose tan is darkest?
Which camp is better,
Malibu, Pine Flats?
I longed to be one of *them*
a Valerie or Susan,
whose long blonde hair
turns green every summer.

At Thirteen I Meet Holden

"Anyway, I keep picturing all these little kids playing some game
in this big field of rye and all . . .And I'm standing on the edge of
some crazy cliff. What I have to do, I have *to catch* everybody if
they start to go over the cliff—"

J.D. Salinger, *The Catcher in the Rye*

While in another room,
my girlfriend screams
at her mother,
I lie with Holden
in a field of white chenille,
whose tufted thread I stroke
with my thumb
as I read about Phoebe, D.B.
The days so long
this summer they poke
from night all endless
and awkward, the way my legs
poke from shorts:
hot, brown, useless.
Days lengthen past bike rides
to Stony Point, past
trips to the pool.
Lengthen into hanging out
with kids I never liked.
My friend and her mother
are *pretty stupid,*
stupider still, my folks at home
having *two hemorrhages apiece*
over some secret I'd told.
I love Holden Caulfield
more than anyone I know.
And I know that a field of rye
will be as soft and cool
as white chenille,
and smell even better than grass
cut from the field next door.
And on that cliff,
higher than Stony Point,
I will be safe.
Holden Caulfield will catch me.

Craving

I broke the long stems
of dry spaghetti
into worm-sized pieces
that I ate as I watched
cartoons on TV:
Baby Huey in his tiny diaper,
Porky and Petunia Pig.
I popped the round top
from the Hershey's chocolate can,
spooned the unsweetened
powder into my mouth.
Mom was pregnant.
At my eleventh birthday party,
Dad patted her belly,
bragged to my friends
that he'd *blown up that balloon.*
It was the beginning of summer.
My friends had begun to kiss boys,
steal candy and cigarettes
from Vons.
I spent the long afternoons
lying on the floor,
cartoons flickering silently
on the black and white TV,
the cord of the telephone
wrapped around my arm,
whispers of the high school boy
I knew from the park
slipping into my ear.
I ate the skin
from the tips of my fingers,
from the tops of my toes
until they bled.
I didn't know then
what was bitter,
as my life spilled out around me,
fine powder from a dark brown tin.

Poem to my First Love

Because our fathers
were too drunk
to pick us up
from the high school dance,
you walked me home
three miles
down dark empty
valley streets,
past tract houses
past orange groves
whose pungent blooms
perfumed the still night air.
I remember your black hair,
green eyes, the cleft
of your chin.
At fifteen, you were
six-foot-four
size fourteen shoe.
Your father beat you
and when he couldn't anymore
drop-kicked you
from the house instead.
In school you were famous
for being handsome, smart,
for football, and lighting
cherry bombs
at lunch time on the quad.
You'd be a doctor, you said
on our slow walk home—
not a plumber
like your father
his life all shit
and tight spaces.
No wonder he'd become
a drunk.

Sweat-Suit

My father lies on the floor
by the open patio door
engaged in an afternoon
snooze. His chest rises
beneath his brown
sweat-suit, carried up
down, by the underground
force of his breath.
Geologic—the bellow, gurgle
of his body at rest.

In the last photograph
he wears that sweat-suit—
cotton thin at the elbows,
knees, showing pin-points
of skin. Thin, like the fabric
of his heart, stretching,
a cheap balloon,
every beat, a beat closer
to its final bursting.

III. Dear Heart

Rank

I never wore white shoes
before Memorial Day
or suede in summer.
I crossed my legs
primly at the ankle,
wore a panty girdle
and a full-length slip,
no shadow of body
apparent through my dress.
I knew better than
to crackle gum,
or walk down the street
cigarette dangling
from my mouth,
knew better than
to pierce my ears,
like some common girl.
Still, his mother
rooted out the tell-tale
signs, traces of a family
line who worked for wages
in "mediocre" jobs.
The day after
we'd spent the night together
and got caught,
he came to my apartment
with a deck of cards
that he spread across
the kitchen table,
saying, Mother says
I have to teach you bridge
so we'll have something
in common.
He arranged the cards
in suits to demonstrate
their ranking,
clubs, diamonds, hearts, spades,
saying spades are the boss
trump, outrank everything,
always.

Dear Heart

I don't remember much of the plot,
but Geraldine Page was a spinster
and Glenn Ford, a traveling salesman,
broke her heart.

As we watched the movie that night
I knew our love was over.
It was the end of spring break
and you were headed back to school.

I cried for days,
getting out of bed just to vomit or pee.
I was wrong, of course; it was only
the beginning.

Green Wedding

I wore the same mint green
crepe dress
I'd worn last summer
to someone else's wedding.
I'd stayed awake till four
in a Seattle Holiday Inn
the night before
the wedding
watching his mother
drink vodka and cry,
while my mother slept
in another room.
Our fathers, at home in L.A.,
too pissed or too cheap
to make the trip.
I was eighteen.
I walked to the altar alone.
The click, click
of my high white pumps
marrying the whish
of pulse in my ear,
my green crepe dress
straining tight
across my chest.

Seattle

"... but Wilson had no car. He felt almost intolerably lonely."
Graham Greene, *The Heart of the Matter*

So homesick I engaged wrong numbers
in conversation
for the sound of another
human voice
 that year in Seattle when it rained three hundred days.
Not hard like it would at home
and then be done for months,
but just a light piss,
air always damp
like the baby's diaper.
I watched pink fingers of mold
double every day
in the corner of the window
looking out on evergreens and endless grass.
I longed for L.A.—
palm trees and hybrid Bermuda,
trees that let in light and grass with grace
enough to die back
yellow in the winter.
I hated the rain the natives praised.
"Rain makes everything green," they'd say,
deranged as they were on chlorophyll and caffeine.
I was green too at nineteen,
with a shiny new husband, one baby,
belly ripening with the next.
My husband studied engineering at the U.
And I studied too—his books from World Lit—
Dostoevski, Kafka, Camus.
My favorite was Graham Greene—
The Power and the Glory, The Heart of the Matter—
burnt-out-cases
adrift in the existential sea.
And I thought then that I
was more displaced
than any whiskey priest or disaffected spy
which I declared to any wrong number
who would take the time
to listen.

Consciousness Raising

Fresh from college
I landed the Big Job:
Conglomerate Electric—
expense account, car.
I dressed for success,
like a man, but with breasts
in a navy blazer, starched blouse,
scarf knotted like a tie
at the neck.

I drove the gray maze of freeway
crisscrossing the basin,
selling *small electrics*
to Savons, The Broadway.
The car was a Plymouth,
AM radio, no air.

Volume up, windows down
I sped the freeways to the Bee Gees
uh uh uh stayin' alive, stayin' alive.
To minimize downtime
I ate lunch while I drove,
foraging my briefcase
for granola bars stashed
with other vital supplies—
spare pantyhose, tampons
and Valium tucked under brochures
for blow dryers.
Rushing to make a dozen calls a day:
to the drug store whose manager
threatened to kill me
if his order came late,
to the warehouse with rats nested
in returned toaster ovens,
to the five and dime
with armed guards

patrolling the aisles,
back to the office where *Hustler*
fold-outs plastered the phone bank,
where my boss drank gin
from a flask at his desk
and daily asked
for a *quickie* in the showroom.

None of my friends were happy
in their new careers.
Some went back to school,
took women's studies
examining their vaginas
with speculum and mirror.
Some joined EST, got their shit together.
Others left their families,
were re-birthed or re-born.
Seventy-nine slouched into eighty,
Reagan elected, John Lennon dead.
No matter how fast I drove
I never got anywhere.
Staying alive
became the only job
I could handle.

Jesus in a Plastic Jacket

My neighbor shows me a picture of Jesus
on the cover of *Time* magazine
he carries with him everywhere
encased in a plastic jacket—
the kind used to keep safe
pages of term papers,
letters from the President or Pope.
"It saved my life," he says.
"Look at the date, my birthday."
He points to the corner,
tells me how he saw Jesus
in the hospital waiting-room
then decided to have the surgery
he'd earlier refused.

Because I saw a horseshoe
on the tail of an airplane I was ticketed
to board one early morning
alone, a continent from home,
I walked across the tarmac,
climbed the stairs.
Afraid to move,
I had looked for a sign
the plane would take me back to Kansas,
not to hell.
And once, wading a vacation ocean,
I met a child
who introduced himself as Jake
and reached for my hand.
Jake. My grandfather's name.
I saw resemblance—
the smile, the same dimple in his chin,
and I thought he'd come back to me
in the form of that black child.
For a moment I believed
I could grasp everything—

the conservation of matter,
the oneness of being,
everlasting life—
hold everything in my hand—
that the lines on my palm
and the freckles on the back
had the same predictive power
as the zodiac,
the same protective balm
as Jesus on the cover of *Time*
encased in a plastic jacket.

IV. Animal, Vegetable, Mineral

February, Los Angeles

The pear tree in the parkway flowers white.

Mockingbird flashes his white blossom
from treetop to fencepost.

The woman says, pear blossoms smelling like semen.
The man says, car alarm in the mockingbird's song.

In this climate, falling blossoms are the only snow.

Mockingbird is king of the night,
as long as he sings, as far as his song reaches.

City of Lakewood

I

City of Lakewood's
orange vested workers chop
jacarandas into stumps.
I see this as I exit the 605
driving east on Del Amo.
The trees strike-slip
the sidewalk with their roots.
I guess this the excuse
to hack the jacarandas
to the ground.
What, come June, will console
us on the gray-gloom days
without the trees'
profligate purple gowns?
But now, it's February.
I turn north on Bloomfield,
enter Cerritos, a newer town,
with parkways of pear trees
in winter white regalia
still years from bursting
concrete with their roots.

II

City of Lakewood
are you jealous of the tree
living in three worlds
at once?

City of Lakewood
do you fear the secret of the tree?
In the democracy of carbon
we are one.

III

City this is that doesn't love a tree.
City of Lakewood.
There is no lake here,
and soon, I fear, no wood.

Vigilance

Picking up Easter lilies
snails severed at the neck,
I understand Mimi
who never left home.

Last week, a girl from my old school
walked into gunfire
on the road I dawdled home on
half a life ago.

Death stayed at home
then, where Lana Turner's daughter
stabbed Johnny Stompanato
and my friend Terry's step-dad
bashed in her dark brown head.
And Helen, after dyeing
her red hair black,
ran away from home.
When her father brought her back,
she ate a hundred aspirin,
went to bed.

I put on gloves
to scatter snail pellets
in the shade of white carnations,
and pick from dirt
the empty shells
whose insides have fizzed
to another place.
Ants climb the gladiola's
tall green pole
and aphids encase
the red hibiscus.
So many yellow leaves,
so many buds falling.

August

August and the flies are slow,
ooze yellow pudding
when squashed
between my palms.
Ants sting my sleep,
crawl across my body
to the ant trap beneath the bed.
Daddy long-legs
rappel from every corner.
Standing on a foot stool,
I broom them down.
When we first moved in,
crickets ruled the house.
To not disturb our luck,
we trapped and placed
each one outdoors.
Soon chirping and jumping
became bad luck enough
and we paid the children
for every cricket killed.
It's easy now
to erase the snails
who eat our basil.
Listen how their shells click—
a wrinkling of paper—
smashing again
against the asphalt street.

Dove

Death mothered beauty
on the sliding glass door
where the ring-necked dove
flew toward the kitchen.
What's left on glass—
more brass rubbing
than fossil—
imprint in feathers and dust,
beak, head, wings
rising slightly in surprise.

Proof

Roses, my dog,
sleeps on her back,
paws raised to the sun,
as if a gift will appear
while she rests.
Tiny miracle of design
lavished underside her paws:
star of black hair
made to pat upon the ground.
Star bounding the four-pad crown
from the soft triangle of flesh.
I think of St. Thomas Aquinas—
the fifth proof for the existence of God—
I'm certain that I do believe in
Roses my dog.

V. Grief Becomes Me

Grief Becomes Me

You've never looked better,
my friends Edward and Neil
tell me and lean close
for a clearer view.
I know what they mean
and believe it's true,
the same way earth and sky
wash to a radiant clean
after relentless days of rain.
How you would present me
with pieces of sea glass
tumbled smooth
from journeying canyons
and rivers to the ocean
and back again
washing up at our feet—
bits of amber, green,
and the rarest stellar blue.
Everything pure and impure
has leached from the soil
of my face,
and in the corners of my eyes,
hard crystals form.

What I Know

Because I awaken
at 6:19
to pain
as if my heart
were a wishbone
pulled apart,
I am not surprised
when they climb
the stairs
to tell me
you are dead.
Now I understand
what fear is:
waiting
for the messenger
to tell me what
I know.

Morning

You come to me in a dream
dressing for your pre-dawn ride,
just as you did on the day
that you died, awakening me
when you turn on the light
to find some missing socks.
I scolded you then,
but now I plead, appeal to reason:
Since you know
what's going to happen
please don't go.
You touch my hair, pull on your jersey,
ride again into that dark morning.

Word

I refuse to say
pass away
or even *die*,
words both passive,
natural, insist
instead on *killed*,
word cruel enough
to pluck you
from this life.

The Dead

One night you come back fat.
When I ask why, you say,
The dead don't exercise,
but we do eat dinner.

Party

I am furious to find
you've planned a gala party
to make up, I guess, for the huge one
that you missed, inviting even guests
who betrayed you after death.
I don't want them in my house,
I scream. But you say, *No harm,*
I'm back now, happy and forgiving
as you were in life.
Angry still, I take up another subject:
If you ride that bike again I will divorce you.
You're not convinced, so I continue:
I'd rather be divorced than have you dead.

Sleep

I fall asleep now in your chair
watching the local late-night news—
other people's tragedies
lulling me to sleep.
On your last night,
exhausted from so much fun—
the swim across the bay,
anniversary wine with friends—
you slept in this chair
until the kids and I hauled you
off to bed, protesting
you were just resting your eyes,
wanted to catch the sports
and then you'd come to bed.

Beach House Facing South

I decorate our new house
as we had planned—
carpet gray as winter ocean,
furniture slip-covered shades of sand—
the same mild scheme
both sides of the window.
Now, I miss the dashes of color
looking out at you
bounding west with our dog
bright in the logo T-shirts that I hated—
two beautiful animals out for fun
in the last heat of summer sun.

Smoke

What would hurt you most
if you look down upon me,
as those who try to comfort
say you do, are the cigarettes
I smoke for solace
mornings when I almost
see you on the beach,
evenings when all I crave
is lost beyond my reach.

Lesson

A portion of ashes we buried,
the portion remaining to be scattered
sits on a shelf
in my office, the container swathed
in a flannel bag, like the bag
protecting your tuxedo shoes.
How handsome you were in formal clothes!
Strangers often asked if you were *someone*.
Should they ask for your autograph?
The irreducible things that make up a person—
ashes, bits of tooth and bone—
transform from one noun
into another.
Before your death, Dear Heart,
I didn't know
that physics and grammar
are the same sad subject:
the transformation of matter,
transforming what matters.

VI. Time, Space ∿

Ring

Josh, in full directness of being four,
says, "Stop wearing that ring,
you're not married anymore."

Even Then

Even in the time unhappiness
washed over me, a flood
that I was helpless to control,
when every night I dreamt of freedom
before we said our old love's dead and gone,
in the time before our new love
bloomed in joy and promise,
even then, Dear Heart,
I never wished for this.

Peninsula

Finger connected to the hand
by an isthmus of land.

I live on one,
travel to another to recover.

Yuke-a-tawn, Jack says, correcting my pronunciation.

At home, the bay on one side,
ocean on the other.

Here, it's ocean and sea.

Peninsula. Might as well be an island
where I've washed up
salty, alone.

Trace

I've given up
underwear, shoes.
I wash my face
but wear no make-up.
My jewelry waits
in a box at home.
My hands are tan now,
betray no trace
of my life before.

Telecast

I watch the *Oscars en Español*
in a pizza joint
under a palapa with Gaba and Drew.
I've seen only two movies
(*Life is Beautiful, Shakespeare in Love*)
in the seven months since your death.

Last year, just days into the new house,
we cooked spaghetti
and watched the telecast with old friends.
We'd seen every movie
(hated *Titanic*, loved *The Full Monty*).
How smug we were in happiness and good taste.

Reef

I never believed
I'd be safe in the sea
without you,
but I risk the half-mile
to the reef and back, float
over purple fans
and hunks of coral
sinuous as the human brain.
Once, in Maui,
I hovered above
as you freed an eel
tethered in strands
of fishing line—
no tools but courage
and your hands.
You never saw an octopus
or squid, though
in waters we traveled
there were many.
Some creatures demand patience
Dear Heart,
but you were restless,
ready to move on.

In Quintana Roo

Kathy gives me a card
with angels on dolphin back
swirling from sea to sky.

I think of the morning last spring
when from our window
we spotted a pod of dolphin
and you abandoned breakfast
to join them for a swim.

The card's inscription: ·
Together we will transcend
the illusion that is time
and space.

Transcend. Joke on my license plate.
Comic motto for the non-believer.
Maybe where you are now
you know what that word means.

Not me. I'm in Mexico.
Interregnum of old life and new.
Angry with you
for this dislocation.
I loved you in my other life.

I dreamt last night my friend
left her green parrot in my care,
but I failed to feed
or give it water
and when she came to claim it,
the bird lay dead
next to a vase of browning lilies.

Suddenly, you appear
in the dark sea
of my dream, saying,
*I don't remember when
we last made love.*

Be patient, Dear Heart,
I'm learning how
to love you dead.